The Magic of C

For Healing and C

Dueep Jyot Singh

Natural Remedy Series

Mendon Cottage Books

JD-Biz Publishing

Download Free Books!

http://MendonCottageBooks.com

All Rights Reserved.

No part of this publication may be reproduced in any form or by any means, including scanning, photocopying, or otherwise without prior written permission from JD-Biz Corp Copyright © 2015

All Images Licensed by Fotolia and 123RF

Disclaimer

The information is this book is provided for informational purposes only. It is not intended to be used and medical advice or a substitute for proper medical treatment by a qualified health care provider. The information is believed to be accurate as presented based on research by the author.

The contents have not been evaluated by the U.S. Food and Drug Administration or any other Government or Health Organization and the contents in this book are not to be used to treat cure or prevent disease.

The author or publisher is not responsible for the use or safety of any diet, procedure or treatment mentioned in this book. The author or publisher is not responsible for errors or omissions that may exist.

Warning

The Book is for informational purposes only and before taking on any diet, treatment or medical procedure, it is recommended to consult with your primary health care provider.

Our books are available at

1. Amazon.com
2. Barnes and Noble
3. Itunes
4. Kobo
5. Smashwords
6. Google Play Books

Table of Contents

Introduction 5

How to Grow Cloves 8

    Growing from Seeds 8

    Time for Germinating 8

    Transplanting Your Seedlings 9

    Water, Water, Everywhere and Not a Drop to Drink… 10

    When Do You Get the Flowers and the Seeds? 10

    When Do You Harvest Them? 11

    Can You Grow Clove Plants from Cuttings? 12

Clove Pomander 13

Clove Oil 15

Cloves in Ancient Remedies 18

    Cloves as Insect Repellent 18

    Suffering from Diarrhea? 19

    Not Feeling Hungry? 20

    Chest Congestion 22

    Throat Infections 22

- Healing Cuts and Bruises 23
  - Clove – Cinnamon Ointment 23
- Cloves in Making Masalas 25
  - Garam Masala 27
  - Lamb Roast with Cloves 29
  - Dal Fry 32
- Anyone for Tempering? 35
- Conclusion 39
  - Winter oil 39
- Author Bio 41
- Publisher 49

Introduction

I remember my father recounting a traditional and ancient Persian poem to me, which he had learned when his grandmother was busy cooking in the kitchen. She was just following ancient traditions, when women from the Mogul times – 14th-century – sang this song for fun in the kitchen, while cooking and amusing their kids at the same time.

The translation from the vernacular goes something like this —

Clove and cardamom – good pals they
Went for a forbidden swim for kicks.
And soon we heard Clove yelling.
"Golly, cardamom has gone for a six[1]".

and so on, in more hilarious verses, about how clove would and could not bother to drag the drowning cardamom out of the water, because he would get wet, catch a cold, his momma had told him not to go swimming, and so on! Until cardamom came out of the water and both went home.

Home, meaning the tummy of a gourmet who would appreciate the presence of cloves and cardamom in his delicately seasoned dish.

The Association of cloves and cardamoms have been a part of the lives of spices in the East. Where you put in a couple of ground cloves, you may be asked whether you want to add some more cardamoms in, too. Most often, you say yes, because after all that is going to increase the taste quotient. Cloves also go well with cinnamon, star anise, basil and pepper.

Nevertheless, this book is going to tell you all about the magic of cloves, which has been considered to be one of the most precious spices treasured down the centuries by the West. Wars were fought for cardamoms, cinnamon, pepper and cloves. Trade routes to the Indies, and to the East were jealously guarded by adventurous traders in the West.

---

[1] Anglo-Indian Slang for out for the count, done for, beyond rescue and reprieve. As in, "Did he get the promotion? No, he went out for a six, when he insulted the boss's GF!" *Official- speak for absolutely no chance of any success in the future however much he may grovel and apologize.*

Cloves first originated in Indonesia from where traders took them all over the world, in ancient times. In fact, 3000 years ago, a Chinese emperor asked his courtiers to chew ding xiang in order to keep their breath fresh, when they came into his presence.

Apart from its use in medicine, it was, and is also used extensively to add taste, sweetness, and warmth to a dish.

Archaeologists have found traces of cloves in archaeological excavations going back to 1721 BC in Syria. So this shows how long this great and precious spice has been associated with mankind.

How to Grow Cloves

Cloves were restricted to just some parts of the East until they were smuggled out in the 16th century by a Frenchman and taken to Zanzibar. However, living in the 21st century, we have easier access to clove plants. So you may want to grow your own clove plant in your garden. Remember that it is a perennial tree. So it is going to need a lot of place to spread. It is the unopened bud of this flower, which is dried and used to spice up your cuisine and your system.

Growing from Seeds

Clove seeds are perishable, and that is why they are not easily available in areas where clove plants are not native. Also, there are plenty of places all over the world, where it is not permitted to import or export clove seeds. So if you can find cloves seeds on eBay, or in your nursery, get them. Do not pack them up in plastic because they are going to dry there. Once the clove seeds get dried, you will never find a clove plant growing.

Clove seeds shipping from Hawaii is illegal. So if you can get the clove fruit with the seeds still inside, get them.

Time for Germinating

You need patience when you are planting these plants. In many cases, these plants have decided to germinate months after they were planted. That depends on the weather.

Cloves seeds are definitely not the dried spices which you are eating. These are buds. Clove seeds are found within the ripe fruit.

Plant the seeds in a well moisturized and well-drained potting medium. Any sort of soil, especially rich, clay and well fertilized soil is welcomed by these plants.

Remember not to cover the seeds with soil at all. The seeds are going to germinate right there on the soil surface when they know that there is fresh air and sun outside.

The clove has to be kept moist. Also, you may place it in partial shade, so that it does not burn up in the heat. Dry soil is fatal to the seed.

Here is one tip which you can use, if you have not had soil prepared, but have received the seeds. Just place them in layers of paper tissue which has been well moistened. Imagine you are sprouting beans. Keep the temperature between 60° and 85°F.

Transplanting Your Seedlings

Cloves start growing roots, before they put out their shoots and leaves. So the moment your cloves start growing these roots, remove them up very carefully, and transplant them when the root are 1 inch in length. These are extremely delicate roots, so tender loving care is needed. Do not let the roots grow too long before you transplant them.

Do not cover the seed cotyledon. Just sprinkle enough of soil around the roots so that they know where to grow. The seed is now going to take firm hold of the soil in the place which is going to be its home, for the next 50-80 years, with any luck.

We are so used to covering seeds, that we plant them ½ - 1 inch below the soil surface. You are so not going to do this with your clove seeds. You cover them, and they are going to say, okay, you want me to go to sleep, because conditions are not conducive to my growing, okay, good night.

And you keep waiting and waiting and waiting, why does not my clove plant grow…

It takes 20 years for you to get a clove crop. That is why these plants are planted by the eldest generation, so that the third-generation can benefit from them. Until then, you can have a beautiful tree, in your garden, adding to the green cover.

Water, Water, Everywhere and Not a Drop to Drink…

If you cannot remove the seeds delicately, I would suggest removing a whole chunk of soil from all around the seed and transplanting that whole soil ball in the chosen place. After you have planted the seed, water it often.

Remember cardamoms are indigenous in places where there is plenty of water around, so they do not mind if the gardener forgot to water them during the day because after all, it rained in the morning and rained in the evening, and rained at suppertime. So do not forget that your little clove loves water, most of the time. Alternating with lots of sunshine.

Of course, the soil is going to be well drained, because you do not want root rot, do you?

When Do You Get the Flowers and the Seeds?

20 years after you first planted your clove, so proudly and saw it beginning to germinate, you can begin to harvest buds which are going to flower. Once they start flowering, you can harvest twice a year. Winter and spring. This is

going to be an annual crop for a number of decades following. So your patience is going to be well rewarded.

When Do You Harvest Them?

The moment the flowers turn purple from their original green color, that is the time when you are going to harvest the flowers. These are then dried in the shade, until they are shriveled up and turn black.

The harvesting process go sometime like this done traditionally throughout the centuries. The buds are removed from the stalks and sun-dried for a week. The buds are dried separately from the stems, because the stems are going to be used for the distillation of clove oil. However, clove oil can also be distilled from the buds even though the percentage is going to be significantly lower.

All of these cloves are raked separately on mats made out of natural fiber or cloth mats, because if they are not put out in the sun as soon as possible, they are going to ferment. And the crop for the year is going to be ruined.

These drying flower buds are turned over periodically so that they dry into a brownish reddish color, which is the clove we appreciate.

Can You Grow Clove Plants from Cuttings?

Yes, you can, that is a good idea if you can get them in your nursery. It is much better and less hassle than growing from seeds.

Only totally dry cloves with absolutely no vestiges of moisture are packed in airtight containers. They are then shipped all over the globe from Zanzibar, Tanzania, India, Indonesia, Java and Sumatra and other Eastern tropical countries.

Clove Pomander

What an excellent Christmas decoration setting idea with pomanders!

In Elizabethan times, aristocrats, who wanted to show off made it a point to have a clove pomander. I can just imagine Gloriana lifting up an orange daintily, and taking a hearty sniff of the cloves, and also cinnamon, in order to show her Royal status, while insinuating that her surroundings and the people around her were odoriferous. Oranges were also very precious at that time in the West.

An orange was taken, shallow cuts were made in the skin, and the cloves were stuck into those cuts until the whole orange was "beaded" with cloves. The Elizabethans, if they had cinnamon around, used to roll the sliced orange in cinnamon powder, before making the surface all hedgehog like with cloves.

This orange was then placed in a dark place, and taken out every day, rotated so that other areas could get shriveled up, – this process took nearly 3 weeks – and once the pomander was done, it was either kept in clothes closets to keep them smelling fresh, or just held in the hand.

Handkerchiefs had not come into existence at that time. So you applied your pomander to your nose whenever you smelled something rotten in the state of Denmark.

Apart from Indonesia, cloves are grown extensively in Zanzibar, also known as the island of cloves, Sri Lanka, India, and Madagascar. Surprisingly enough, the world's largest producer is an island, off the Tanzanian coast, called Pemba.

Clove Oil

Clove Oil is normally extracted by subjecting the dried clove buds and portions of the dried stem to steam distillation. The eugenol percentage in this oil is 85%. That is why it is a very strong and powerful oil and has to be used in minute quantities.

How many times have you found yourself with a raging toothache, and you do not want to go to a doctor. Well, did not grandma just dip a cotton ball in clove oil, and tell you to bite on it? Well, clove oil does not heal the pain. It just deadens the sensation in the skin, and you think that you have got complete relief, until you find yourself waking up with your tooth playing Merry pranks in your mouth at 2 o'clock the next night.

Nevertheless, clove oil was considered to be a good"cure" for tooth ache since ancient times, and many of us still believe that. The real truth is that you will need to get your tooth seen to, by an experienced dentist, because it needs care and cleaning.

Clove oil is a short-term remedy. You can get the same skin deadening effect by rubbing a paste of black pepper over that area. No wonder clove oil and black pepper oil is often used as a pain relief ingredient in natural massage lotions and ointments.

Rubbing too much of clove oil on affected gums and teeth can have a detrimental effect on the tissue surrounding that area. I suffered from clove oil burns just about a week ago, when I rubbed that oil over a tooth paining because of the cold. That oil seeped to the side of my mouth and "burnt" it. It took five days to heal.

So do not use pure clove oil in large quantities. You do not want the tissues in your mouth and cheeks start to yowl, even though your tooth has stopped nagging you to go see a dentist, see a dentist.

So tip based on bitter experience – Remember to dilute the few drops of clove oil with water, and allow to get absorbed in the piece of cotton, before you plug that aching tooth with this short-term remedy.

The delicious clove taste found in this spice is due to an aromatic named eugenol. This is also very powerful and that is why you are told that cloves have a "warming" and "hot" effect on your body. So you never add more than one or two cloves in a dish in its powdered form.

Cloves in Ancient Remedies

Ancient Indian, Chinese, and Tibetan medicine used cloves extensively. However, they were not encouraged in the summer, because they are considered to be of a warm nature. However, they are used extensively in the winter in herbal teas and to prevent coughs and colds. That is why people suffering or who are genetically more prone to autoimmune diseases are not advised to eat cloves.

Cloves as Insect Repellent

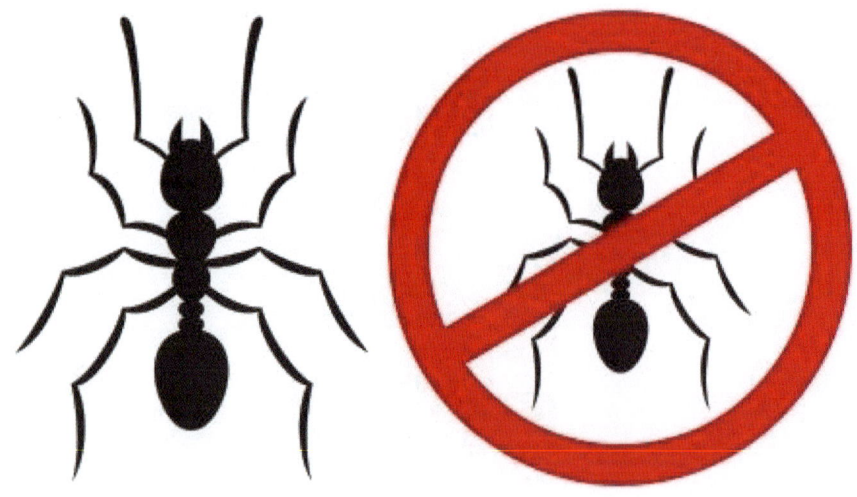

This comes in the category of grandma's natural remedies, because the clove has been used since centuries for repelling insects, including ants. That is because of the powerful aroma of the clove oil. So if you want to get rid of ants, in your kitchen, just place a couple of crushed cloves on a lid in the area, which shows plenty of ant activity. This is soon going to make all the ants disappear from that particular area.

You may also want to powder some cloves and place them in small cloth bundles. Hang these cloth bundles in your cupboards or place them in any place where you find silverfish, moths and other insects moving around. There, you have got rid of them without any resort to pesticides which are going to be potentially harmful to you and your family.

Suffering from Diarrhea?

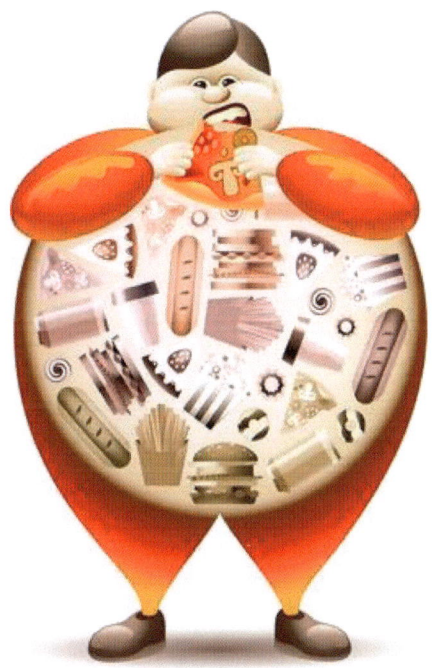

Digestive problems are often caused by eating too much or too rich food.

Take two drops of clove oil in half a teaspoonful of honey. Drink this twice a day, if you are suffering from diarrhea. Drink this only once, a day, if you are suffering from indigestion.

So cloves in different proportions can heal two different ailments.

In the same way, indigestion can also be cured by drinking two ground cloves in a glass full of warm water.

Not Feeling Hungry?

Stress and tension can cause a loss of appetite.

You may find you losing your appetite due to many reasons, including stress, strain, tension, or if you are recuperating from an illness.

Make up a mixture of grinding 3 g each of dried ginger, rock salt, bishops weed and clove together. 3 g is half a teaspoon. Take half a teaspoon of this yummy appetizer, twice a day and you are soon going to find yourself regaining your appetite.

This is because the cloves have woken up your digestive system and the ginger has helped to cure any possible potential infections in your tummy.

In the same way, if you are suffering from weakness, brought about by fever, just add two cloves to the drinking water, which you drink. This water needs to be boiled to prevent any other infections and the cloves are going to help heal you.

When I was living in the South of India as a child, this same ancient tradition of boiling water with some spice in it – cumin in this case – was practiced extensively, and that was the water, which was drunk throughout the day by all the members of the family.

Many of the families had traditional copper, and even silver drinking utensils. But then, South India has always been the land of ancient tradition going down millenniums and because it was not often subjected to invasions by mid-Asian invaders, it managed to keep its riches, traditions, rituals, practices, and customs mostly intact, coming down the ages.

The matriarch of the family used to get up early in the morning and while the younger females prepared the breakfast, ground coffee for the family, the eldest lady used to boil water with roasted powdered cumin seeds, and then place them into different water containers throughout the house.

So you could not go anywhere without easy access to some water source. So, what a nice way to make sure that your family never suffers from dehydration and also make sure that all the containers were finished by nighttime.

In this way, children got used to drinking water throughout the day, and often. I never found any of those children suffering from toxic problems, either as children are as adults because their systems were well hydrated with antiseptic water. So whether you use cloves, or you use cumin, add these spices to your drinking water and keep healthy.

Also, clove water is effective to get rid of worms in your tummy.

Chest Congestion

Roast three cloves on the griddle, and powder them. Now take this powder with half a teaspoon of honey before you go to sleep. This is going to help relieve chest congestion, and also help in curing potential just problems.

Throat Infections

You do not need to suffer from a stuffy nose and a throat infection, if you have cloves around.

I found that two roasted cloves kept in your mouth throughout the day not only kept your mouth and breath fresh, but it also helped produce enough of moisture and clove oil to eliminate nasty phlegm, and any irritation in your throat. Try it out. It is worth it. Especially in the winters.

Also, another tip. This was extremely efficacious when I found my throat getting hoarse after continuous talking for about 4 to 5 hours during training sessions. Also, it gave me a chance to keep quiet!

To make this even more palatable, I sprinkled the little bit of clove powder on honey and licked the spoon – cannot resist honey – before I popped the cloves into the gab box.

Ready for next talkathon session, within half an hour.

Healing Cuts and Bruises

I wonder why more people do not use this perfect combination to get rid of cuts , open wounds and bruises, without scarring? Turmeric is the necessary ingredient here, which is going to prevent scarring.

Clove – Cinnamon Ointment

Make up my natural ointment right now and put it in your healing closet.

Half a cup of coconut oil.

Half a cup of wheat germ/olive oil/almond oil. [All these oils are extremely amazingly good healing agents.]

¼ cup beeswax.

4 tablespoons turmeric powder.

1 teaspoon cardamom powder.

Half teaspoon cinnamon powder.

Four teaspoons cloves powder.

Take a double boiler, and place the oils, as well as the beeswax in the inner container. Now place water in the outer container. Stir constantly and heat on slow heat until the wax melts, and the oil begins to give you an ointment like consistency. Now add all the spices. Stir until they are thoroughly mixed.

You may want to thicken the ointment. Add more wax. For thinning, add more oil. For more power, add more cinnamon and cloves.

Place in a glass jar and the next time you find yourself suffering from cuts, just apply a little bit of this ointment after cleaning that hurt area thoroughly. Turmeric prevents that area from scarring after it has been healed.

Okay, let me admit it. I could not resist putting in a teaspoonful of honey in the last batch I made. Well, it has been in use for the past six months, and my skin is totally scar free. Even though I keep scratching and hurting it ever so often during my rather gawky accident prone existence.

Cloves in Making Masalas

This traditional meat dish is going to have cloves in it, in some form or the other, either fried with the original onion and garlic and tomato masala or as a last sprinkling of garam masala

If you are interested in Eastern cuisine, you may have heard of spice mixes, where you are immediately told to make up a garam masala and add a teaspoonful, to give you the authentic Eastern curry taste, especially in Indian cuisine.

This is a stopgap measure for all those people, who do not have the time or the energy to make this masala fresh every day. This is what is normally done in Eastern kitchens. Even today, the lady of the house takes out 5 g each of all these spices, and then she grinds them together after she has roasted them on the griddle.

The family cook always insisted on a pestle and mortar, because he was very particular about taste, proportions and textures, and roughly ground spices but I use the coffee grinder to get the finer powder. That is when I do not have the original spices around. Cloves are necessarily an integral part of this masala.

All of these different curry powders and curry mixes cannot manage without cloves.

I remember a gourmet uncle of mine doling out these spices to his cook for lunch, because he was very particular about the amount and the proportions of the spices, which went in making his very appreciated meals more aromatic and delicious. Well, here is the traditional recipe of the garam masala that you buy in the market today.

You are going to use it just by sprinkling a little bit of this masala on the food after it has been cooked, and it is ready to serve. Many cooks use a teaspoonful of this masala as a substitute for a mixture of spices, but that makes the Curry taste extra spicy.

A curry should be actually mildly subtle in taste with the minimum of masalas used. But if it is being overpowered by a teaspoonful of garam masala – as is the wont of many cooks pretending to be traditional Indian cooks online – half of the fun of that original curry taste is gone.

Garam Masala

Garam masala literally means hot mixture. So the basic garam masala recipe is going to be made up of

6 tablespoons each freshly ground black pepper and roasted coriander seeds, 5 tablespoons black cumin seeds roasted and ground, 1 ½ teaspoons each ground cinnamon and ground cloves, 1 tablespoon ground mace, 1 teaspoon black mustard seeds, ¼ teaspoon fenugreek powder, 2 ½ tablespoons ground cardamom seeds and 2 tablespoons ground bay leaf. You may also want to add some rock salt to it to give it a spicy taste.

All the spices are ground very fine, or medium fine if you prefer it. Keep in an airtight jar. This is not a curry powder and can be used on its own, though it is going to blend very well with any other aromatics used in your cuisine.

Use it for grills, barbecues, skewered and sauté meat and vegetables. If you are using it in curries, you sprinkle this masala on the surface of the dish during the last five minutes of cooking.

You may find many supposedly authentic recipes calling for one spoon garam masala to be added to the dish. Unfortunately, that has become the trend with many enthusiastic cooks turned authorities on cooking, who are looking for shortcuts in making traditional dishes. This garam masala needs to be sprinkled on your cooked food, and not used as a fried curry powder.

Meat is delicious, especially when you are getting ready to roast it, if it has been marinated before with powdered cloves, ginger, paprika and garlic. I noticed that cinnamon and cardamoms do not have that same powerful effect as cloves have when partnered with meat in the initial stages of cooking. These two spices are best added during cooking or as a sprinkle, after the cooking has been done.

Lamb Roast with Cloves

This is marinated, roasted and then served with parsley or other greens.

This is the traditional recipe in which you are going to be using a leg of lamb or pork with the fat and the skin removed.

This is for six hungry people, and you are going to prepare it in 20 minutes. The marinating time is 48 hours! Why so much time? Because you are going to steep it in the marinade, with all the spices so that you have juicy spicy meat at the end of the day to serve up on a special occasion.

So if you are preparing this for a feast, remember it has to be marinated 48 hours in advance.

Cooking time is four hours. You will also need one hour standing time.

2.5 kg of lamb leg, with the fat and the skin removed
The marinade is going to consist of
150 g of natural yogurt.
1 tablespoon full of salt.
1 teaspoon turmeric powder.
2 teaspoons of roasted and ground cumin seeds
50 g of fresh chopped root ginger
Six cloves of garlic.
Rind of one lemon
8 tablespoons of lemon juice
Six cardamoms crushed
½ teaspoon of ground cloves

Extras –
4 tablespoons brown sugar
5 ounces of unpeeled almonds
1 teaspoon of saffron threads soaking in 3 tablespoons of boiling water – this is just to add extra luxury to your dish if it is a party dish. If you

are making it for an ordinary dinner, you can safely leave out the saffron, as well as the almonds.

Parsley for garnishing .

Make up the marinade by mixing all the marinade items – ginger, lemon rind, garlic, and juice, salt, spices in the food processor.

Prick the lamb with a fork and then make gashes in the flesh in 12 deep cuts.

Soak the marinade all over the land, and leave to stand for one hour in a casserole.

Combine 4 tablespoons of almonds with yogurt and 2 tablespoons full of sugar. Stir in the yogurt and pour over the lamb. Cover the casserole tightly and leave to marinade for 48 hours in the refrigerator.

When you are ready to cook the lamb, preheat the oven to Gas Mark Seven – 425°F – 220° centigrade.

The meat has to reach room temperature before you start cooking it. Sprinkle the remaining sugar over the meat and cook it uncovered in the oven for 30 minutes.

Lower the temperature to Gas Mark Three – 160°C – 325°F and allow the roast to cook in a covered pan for three hours, basting it occasionally with marinade juice, yogurt or butter, if you want. Sprinkle the saffron water over the cooking meat and cook for another 30 minutes or until it is tender.

Remove the meat from the pan, and wrap it up in foil. Skim off all the fat from the casserole and boil the sauce until it is cooked and thick.

Place the meat on a dish and pour the sauce over it. Garnish with parsley, before serving. You may want to accompany this with boiled potatoes and peas.

Dal Fry

I am now introducing you to the staple traditional diet dish of a large percentage of people all over the Indian subcontinent. Indians were basically vegetarian down the millenniums , and that is why they got their nutrition and proteins from lentils, which are also known as dals.

This lentils dish was then highly spiced with garlic, onion, spices and lemon juice. No lunch or dinner is considered complete without some sort of lentils dish. And thanks to the amazing variety of beans and dals available in the

East, these are fast to cook, good to eat, highly nutritious, extremely delicious and a good dish for your meals.

The lentils, which are going to be used in this particular dish is called masur. Muh –soor. It is red in color, but turns yellow, when it is cooked. You normally wash it, and soak it for 20 minutes before cooking. Lentils are rich in carbohydrates, proteins, iron and phosphorus as well as the vitamin B's group.

So if you do not have meat around, try the flavor of spicy masur dal.

For this protein filled healthy dish you need 4 tablespoons full of oil. Traditionally, this is tempered in clarified butter, also known as desi ghee.
Six cloves, six cardamoms, one chopped onion, 1 inch piece of chopped root ginger
1 inch piece of cinnamon.
Two cloves of chopped garlic
Half a teaspoonful of garam masala – I am breaking my rule and telling you to take half a teaspoonful of garam masala here, because I am mixing all the spices together.
250 g lentils – wash and soak them for 20 minutes.
4 tablespoons full of lemon juice, salt to taste.
Two – three Dried chilies, chopped and seeded. I normally use green chilies.

Heat the oil in your cooking wok. Add the cardamoms and cloves, as well as the cinnamon and fry until they start to swell.

Add the onion and fry until it is golden brown. Now add the garlic, garam masala, ginger and chili and cook for about five minutes.

Add the washed and soaked lentils. Stir and fry for one minute. Add the salt to taste, and enough of water to cover about 1 ½ inches above the level of the lentils. Bring this to a boil and simmer for about 20 minutes, until the lentils are tender and thick.

Sprinkle with the lemon juice, stir and serve immediately with boiled rice or roti. You may want to garnish with coriander and onion rings. Remember not to overcook this dish, because then you are going to get a glutinous yellow mass which could pass off as a soup with a little bit of water added!

Anyone for Tempering?

Now this portion is for the really adventurous who want something hot and spicy. This is called tempering. It is done with desi ghee. Gather the people around you because this is going to be served burning hot, right in the Wok.

Take 3 tablespoons full of desi ghee, and put them on the fire. Take some mustard seeds, a touch of asafoetida, and some nigella seeds. Throw them into the hot oil, till they splutter in indignation.

This red hot ghee mixture is poured right over the dal, and it is served sizzling noisily to the hungry brood gathered on your table.

This tempering is called Tadka , and is also done to meat. But that is done with Desi ghee and red chilies.

Put the desi ghee on the heat, and when it is red hot, throw in half a teaspoonful of chili powder. And then pour in the meat. I normally switch off the fire, when I am throwing in the chili powder, because the meat, which is going to come next is going to catch fire, thanks to the chili powder and desi ghee fumes. Also, this Tadka gives the last tempering glaze to the meat or to the dal. Stir and serve right in that same cooking utensil. It is then eaten boiling hot.

My father had an old ancient traditional copper bowl called a *baati*. As opposed to balti- Wok/bucket.

We used to gather around him to see him doing the Tarka on the meat cooked by our cook or by our grandmother.

The moment the chilies started to smoke, we kids knew what would be coming next. The kitchen stove on fire! Dad never switched the fire off.

However, the fire used to extinguish itself within a minute, because our kitchen was well ventilated and there was no inflammable materials around.

And we had red hot, delicious , spicy tarka meat to eat. Nice!

Do not try out this experiment, because chance-taking father is an experienced if amateur chef who enjoys showmanship even if it is in his own kitchen! I am not of his experience, expertise or quality, and possibly you are also not one. So why take a chance of your kitchen range catching fire?

I am giving you the recipe of how to make Desi Ghee right at home, because I am not very sure about the products found in the market.

Desi ghee is clarified butter, which is extremely concentrated and a very powerful healing agent. It is normally used in the making up of herbal medicines, because it is made of pure creamy milk butter. It is also used in making beauty creams, potions, lotions and other skin ointments.

It has a powerful aroma, and that is why only just a spoonful is added to fry meats. It is going to float on the surface of the meat dish, after it has been cooked, so you need to stir the gravy before serving. Also, the food is not going to taste greasy, even though it looks like it has been swimming in fat.

Desi ghee is the concentrated form of pure butter, which is heated to reduce the butter of all the impurities as well as moisture. This concentrated butter is normally used in Eastern cuisine, for searing meat, sautéing and frying food, because they offer its higher burning point. You make this at home by taking 2 pounds of best unsalted butter and melting it in a heavy bottomed pan.

Allow the butter to liquefy on low heat for about 40 minutes. Maintain this simmering point, until all of the moisture in the butter has evaporated. The impurities are going to sink to the bottom of the pan. Remember to keep stirring the butter, so that it does not burn.

Pour off the clear butter and strain it through several thicknesses of muslin cloth. This butter is going to last for about a year, if it is placed in a cool and dry place. This butter is exorbitantly expensive. So in the East, people with easy access to plenty fresh milk make it right in their kitchens for crisp delicious frying results, and adding that taste of pure butter to all their dishes.

Conclusion

Now that you know more about the healing properties and the use of closing cuisine, you may find yourself using it more to keep you healthy.

Remember too much of clove oil is detrimental to your skin tissue. So always that you did, and use it in small quantities.

When you are trying to get rid of some pain, you can use clove oil to deaden that particular area. That is why clove oil along with eucalyptus oil, peppermint oil, oil of Wintergreen, and cinnamon oil along with red chillies and a little bit of cardamom oil mixed together, is used as a massaging rubefacient in winter to get relief from joint pain and other muscle related and bone related ailments.

Winter oil

Here are the proportions – 15 drops Eucalyptus oil, 12 drops of oil of Wintergreen, three drops each of clove oil, peppermint oil, cardamom oil and cinnamon oil with two drops of chili oil. Mix them together and place them in the sun – the winter sun. This is milder.

Allow them to sun themselves for two days. Then take a very little bit of this oil and add this to 1 cup of coconut oil, or almond oil. Now it has been diluted enough to be used as a massaging oil.

Massage on the affected area once every day, gently for about 10 to 15 minutes. This is going to give you pain relief and help make your joints supple.

Add dried fruit and fenugreek to your diet in the winter, if you are suffering from joint pain. You may also want to drink a pinch of cinnamon powder, a pinch of cardamom powder and two hefty pinches of clove powder in a glass full of hot milk twice a day – during the winter only.

See how much easier life is with the magic of spices, including, cloves to keep you healthy and ailments – free.

Live Long and Prosper.

Author Bio

Dueep Jyot Singh is a Management and IT Professional who managed to gather Postgraduate qualifications in Management and English and Degrees in Science, French and Education while pursuing different enjoyable career options like being an hospital administrator, banker, IT,SEO and HRD Database Manager/ trainer, movie scriptwriter, theatre artiste and public speaker, lecturer in French, Marketing and Advertising, ex-Editor of Hearts On Fire (now known as Solstice) Books Missouri USA, advice columnist and cartoonist, publisher and Aviation School trainer, ex-moderator on Medico.in, banker, student councilor ,travelogue writer … among other things!

One fine morning, she decided that she had enough of killing herself by Degrees and went back to her first love -- writing. It's more enjoyable! She already has 48 published academic and 14 fiction- in- different- genre books under her belt.

When she is not designing websites or making Graphic design illustrations for clients , she is browsing through old bookshops hunting for treasures, of which she has an enviable collection – including R.L. Stevenson, O.Henry, Dornford Yates, Maurice Walsh, C.N.Williamson, Sapper, Bartimeus and the crown of her collection- Dickens "The Old Curiosity Shop," and so on… Just call her "Renaissance Woman" - collecting herbal remedies, acting like Universal Helping Hand/Agony Aunt, or escaping to her dear mountains for a bit of exploring, collecting herbs and plants, and trekking.

Check out some of the other Health Learning Series books at Amazon.com

[Health Learning Series on Amazon](#)

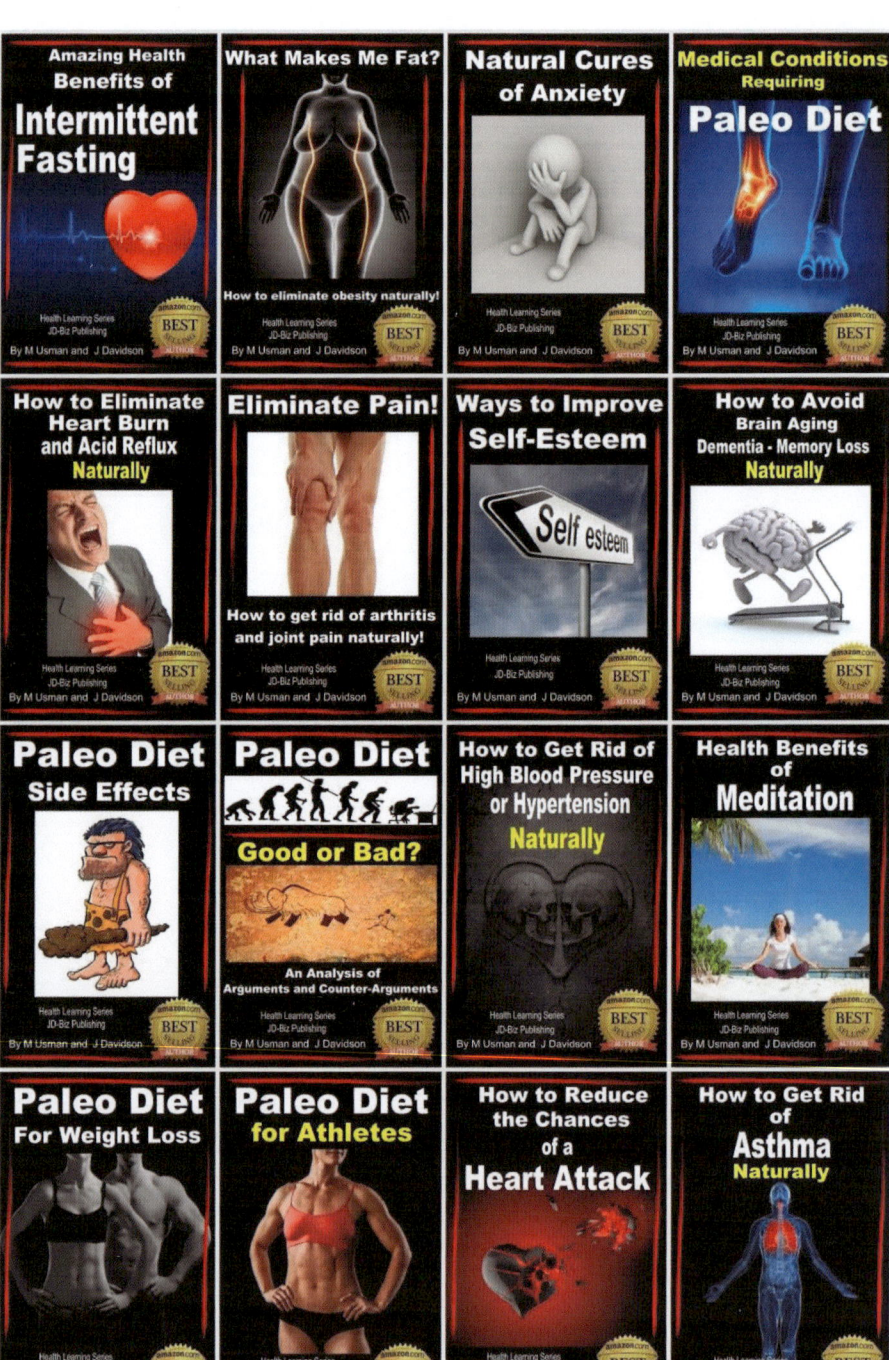

Amazing Animal Books Series

Learn To Draw Series

How to Build and Plan Books

Our books are available at

1. Amazon.com
2. Barnes and Noble
3. Itunes
4. Kobo
5. Smashwords
6. Google Play Books

Download Free Books!

http://MendonCottageBooks.com

Publisher

JD-Biz Corp

P O Box 374

Mendon, Utah 84325

http://www.jd-biz.com/

Printed in Great Britain
by Amazon